CW00368832

Three Chord Tricks

Wise Publications
London/New York/Paris/Sydney/Copenhagen/Madrid

Also available...

Three Chord Tricks: The Blue Book

Twenty-one more hit songs...

Achy Breaky Heart Billy Ray Cyrus
All Along The Watchtower Bob Dylan/Jimi Hendrix
All Right Now Free
Big Yellow Taxi Joni Mitchell
Brown Eyed Girl Van Morrison
Bye Bye Love The Everly Brothers
Cecilia Simon & Garfunkel
Common People Pulp
Get Back The Beatles
Get It On (Bang A Gong) T Rex
I Still Haven't Found What I'm Looking For U2
I'm Still Remembering The Cranberries
In The Air Tonight Phil Collins
Jolene Dolly Parton
Julie The Levellers
Lay Down Sally Eric Clapton
Lily The Pink The Scaffold
Love Me Do The Beatles
Memphis Tennessee Chuck Berry
Mersey Paradise The Stone Roses
Rivers Of Babylon Boney M
Order No. AM951379

Exclusive Distributors:
Music Sales Limited
8-9 Frith Street,
London W1V 5TZ, England.
Music Sales Pty Limited
120 Rothschild Avenue,
Rosebery, NSW 2018,
Australia.

Order No. AM951380
ISBN 0-7119-7242-7
This book © Copyright 1998 by Wise Publications

Compiled by Peter Evans
Music arranged by Rikky Rooksby
Music processed by The Pitts
Cover design by Studio Twenty, London

Printed in the United Kingdom by
Caligraving Limited, Thetford, Norfolk.

Your Guarantee of Quality
As publishers, we strive to produce every book to the
highest commercial standards.
This book has been carefully designed to minimise awkward
page turns and to make playing from it a real pleasure.
Particular care has been given to specifying acid-free,
neutral-sized paper made from pulps which have not been
elemental chlorine bleached. This pulp is from farmed
sustainable forests and was produced with special regard
for the environment.
Throughout, the printing and binding have been planned
to ensure a sturdy, attractive publication which should
give years of enjoyment.
If your copy fails to meet our high standards, please
us and we will gladly replace it.

Music Sales' complete catalogue describes thousands of
titles and is available in full colour sections by subject,
direct from Music Sales Limited. Please state your areas
of interest and send a cheque/postal order for £1.50
for postage to: Music Sales Limited, Newmarket Road,
Bury St. Edmunds, Suffolk IP33 3YB.

Amazing Grace Judy Collins **6**
Blowin' In The Wind Bob Dylan **8**
Brimful Of Asha Cornershop **10**
C'mon Everybody Eddie Cochran **14**
El Condor Pasa (If I Could) Simon & Garfunkel **13**
Eleanor Rigby The Beatles **16**
Free To Decide The Cranberries **20**
Going Down The Stone Roses **22**
Johnny B. Goode Chuck Berry **24**
Long Tall Sally Little Richard **26**
Me And Julio Down By The Schoolyard Paul Simon **28**
Mr Tambourine Man Bob Dylan/The Byrds **30**
Mull Of Kintyre Wings **33**
Oh Boy Buddy Holly **34**
Paperback Writer The Beatles **36**
Ride A White Swan T.Rex **48**
Rock Around The Clock Bill Haley and His Comets **40**
Spice Up Your Life Spice Girls **42**
Still Water The Four Tops **44**
The First Cut Is The Deepest Cat Stevens/Rod Stewart **18**
The Mighty Quinn Bob Dylan/Manfred Mann **38**
Walk Of Life Dire Straits **46**

Introduction **4**
Playing Guide: Relative Tuning/Reading Chord Boxes **5**

The Three Chord Trick songbooks
allow even the beginner guitarist to build
a repertoire of rock classics.
Simply by mastering the three chords used in any of these
songs, you really could play in a day...perhaps even less!
And once you know them, you're on the way to being a
fully-fledged performer.
This songbook doesn't use musical notation, instead you just
learn three easy-to-read chord boxes.
Many popular songs only use three chords.
The most common formula is the 'three-chord trick',
using the three primary chords of any major key.
So in G this would be G, C, and D.
Many rock'n'roll numbers and Dylan's folk-inspired
songs use only these chords.

Three Chord Tricks

Throughout the book chord boxes are printed at the
head of each song; the chord changes are shown
above the lyrics. It's left up to you, the guitarist,
to decide on a strum rhythm or picking pattern.
You might find the pitch of the vocal line is not always
comfortable because it is pitched too high or too low.
In that case, you can change the key without learning
a new set of chords; simply place a capo
behind a suitable fret.
Whatever you do, this three-chord songbook
guarantees hours of enjoyment for
the prospective guitarist.

Relative Tuning

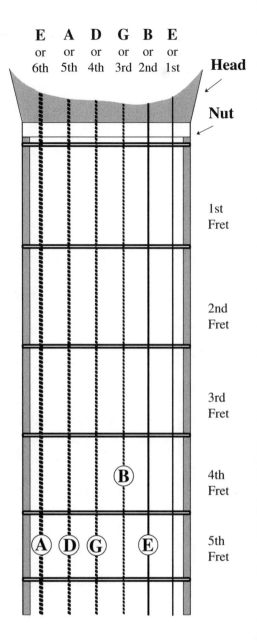

The guitar can be tuned with the aid of pitch pipes or dedicated electronic guitar tuners which are available through your local music dealer. If you do not have a tuning device, you can use relative tuning. Estimate the pitch of the 6th string as near as possible to E or at least a comfortable pitch (not too high, as you might break other strings in tuning up). Then, while checking the various positions on the diagram, place a finger from your left hand on the:

5th fret of the E or 6th string and **tune the open A**(or 5th string) to the note (A)

5th fret of the A or 5th string and **tune the open D** (or 4th string) to the note (D)

5th fret of the D or 4th string and **tune the open G** (or 3rd string) to the note (G)

4th fret of the G or 3rd string and **tune the open B** (or 2nd string) to the note (B)

5th fret of the B or 2nd string and **tune the open E** (or 1st string) to the note (E)

Reading Chord Boxes

Chord boxes are diagrams of the guitar neck viewed head upwards, face on as illustrated. The top horizontal line is the nut, unless a higher fret number is indicated, the others are the frets.

The vertical lines are the strings, starting from E (or 6th) on the left to E (or 1st) on the right.

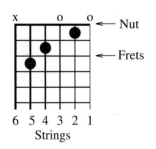

The black dots indicate where to place your fingers.

Strings marked with an O are played open, not fretted.

Strings marked with an X should not be played.

Amazing Grace

Traditional

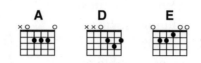

Verse 1

  A   D   A
Amazing grace, how sweet the sound
              E
That saved a wretch like me,
  A   D   A
I once was lost but now I'm found,
       E A
Was blind but now I see.

Verse 2

      A   D   A
'Twas grace that taught my heart to fear
           E
And grace my fear relieved,
     A   D   A
How precious did that grace appear,
       E A
The hour I first believed.

Verse 3

      A   D   A
Through many dangers, toils and fears
         E
We have already come,
     A   D   A
'Twas grace that brought us safe thus far,
      E   A
And grace will lead us home.

Verse 4

     A   D   A
When we've been there ten thousand years,
        E
Bright shining as the sun,
    A   D   A
We've no less days to sing God's praise
      E   A
Than when we first began.

Verse 5

       A   D   A
Amazing grace, how sweet the sound
                        E
That saved a wretch like me,
   A   D   A
I once was lost but now I'm found,
          E   D   A
Was blind but now I see. ——

Blowin' In The Wind

Words & Music by Bob Dylan

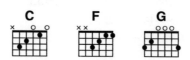

Verse 1

C   F   C
How many roads must a man walk down
      F   C G
Before you call him a man?
     C   F   C
Yes, 'n' how many seas must a white dove sail
      F   G
Before she sleeps in the sand?
     C   F   C
Yes, 'n' how many times must the cannon balls fly
      F C
Before they're forever banned?

Chorus 1

    F   G   C
The answer, my friend, is blowin' in the wind,
    F   G   C
The answer is blowin' in the wind.

Verse 2

C   F   C
How many times must a man look up
      F   C G
Before he can see the sky?
     C   F   C
Yes, 'n' how many ears must one man have
      F   G
Before he can hear people cry?
     C   F   C
Yes, 'n' how many deaths will it take 'til he knows
      F   C
That too many people have died?

Chorus 2

    F   G   C
The answer, my friend, is blowin' in the wind,
    F   G   C
The answer is blowin' in the wind.

Verse 3

<pre>
C   F   C
How many years can a mountain exist
             F   C   G
Before it's washed to the sea?
           C   F   C
Yes, 'n' how many years can some people exist
                  F   G
Before they're allowed to be free?
           C   F   C
Yes, 'n' how many times can a man turn his head
                F   C
Pretending he just doesn't see?
</pre>

Chorus 3

<pre>
            F   G   C
The answer, my friend, is blowin' in the wind,
     F   G   C
The answer is blowin' in the wind.
     F   G   C
The answer is blowin' in the wind.
</pre>

Brimful Of Asha

Words & Music by Tjinder Singh

A   E   D

(chord diagrams)

Intro

‖: A | E D | A | E D :‖

Verse 1

       A   E   D
There's dancing behind movie scenes,
           A   E   D
Behind the movie scenes Sadi Rani,
A   E   D
She's the one that keeps the   dream alive
           A   D
From the morning past the evening
         A
To the end of the light.

Chorus 1

      (A)   E   D
Brimful of Asha on the forty-five,
         A   E   D
Well it's a brimful of Asha on the forty-five.
A   E   D
Brimful of Asha on the forty-five,
         A   E   D
Well it's a brimful of Asha on the forty-five.

Link

‖: A | E D | A | E D :‖

Verse 2

       A   E   D
And singing, illuminate the main streets
         A   E   D
And the cinema aisles,
A   E   D
We don't care about no government warnings
         A   D
'Bout their promotion of the simple life
         A
And the dams they're building.

Chorus 2	As Chorus 1

Bridge 1	A D	

A   **D**
Everybody needs a bosom for a pillow,

A   **D**
Everybody needs a bosom.

A   **D**
Everybody needs a bosom for a pillow,

A   **D**
Everybody needs a bosom.

A   **D**
Everybody needs a bosom for a pillow,

A   **D**
Everybody needs a bosom.

Mine's on the forty-(five.)

Link   ‖: **A** | **E** **D** | **A** | **E** **D** :‖
              five.

Verse 3

A   **E**   **D**
Mohamid Rufi. (Forty-five.)

A   **E**   **D**
Lata Mangeskar. (Forty-five.)

A   **E**   **D**
Solid state radio. (Forty-five.)

A   **E**   **D**
Ferguson mono. (Forty-five.)

A   **E**   **D**
Bon Publeek. (Forty-five.)

A   **D**
Jacques Dutronc and the Bolan Boogie,

    A   **D**
The Heavy Hitters and the chi-chi music,

A   **E**   **D**
All India Radio. (Forty-five.)

A   **E**   **D**
Two-in-ones. (Forty-five.)

A   **E**   **D**
Argo records. (Forty-five.)

A   **E**   **D**
Trojan records. (Forty-five.)

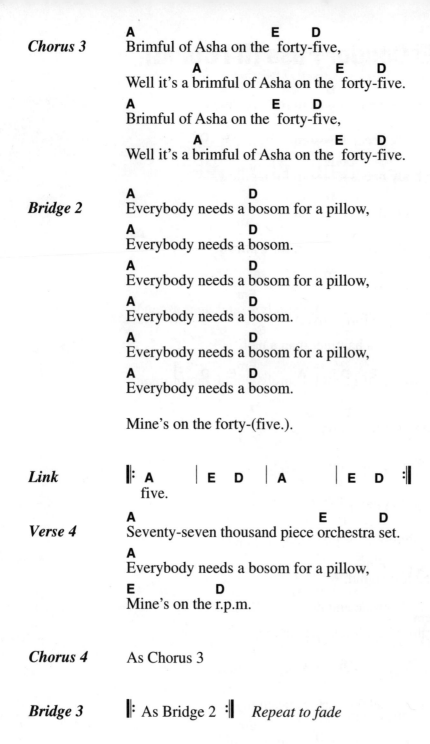

Chorus 3

    A   E   D
Brimful of Asha on the forty-five,

                A   E   D
Well it's a brimful of Asha on the forty-five.

    A   E   D
Brimful of Asha on the forty-five,

                A   E   D
Well it's a brimful of Asha on the forty-five.

Bridge 2

A   D
Everybody needs a bosom for a pillow,

A   D
Everybody needs a bosom.

A   D
Everybody needs a bosom for a pillow,

A   D
Everybody needs a bosom.

A   D
Everybody needs a bosom for a pillow,

A   D
Everybody needs a bosom.

Mine's on the forty-(five.).

Link

‖: A | E D | A | E D :‖
    five.

Verse 4

A   E   D
Seventy-seven thousand piece orchestra set.

A
Everybody needs a bosom for a pillow,

E   D
Mine's on the r.p.m.

Chorus 4   As Chorus 3

Bridge 3   ‖: As Bridge 2 :‖   *Repeat to fade*

El Condor Pasa (If I Could)

Musical Arrangement by J. Milchberg & D. Robles
English Lyric by Paul Simon

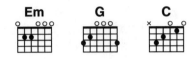

Intro **Em** *ad lib*

Verse 1
    Em   **G**
I'd rather be a sparrow than a snail,
                      Em
Yes I would, if I could, I surely would, mmm-mm.
                   G
I'd rather be a hammer than a nail,
                      Em
Yes I would, if I could, I surely would, mmm-mm.

Bridge
  C
Away, I'd rather sail away
    G
Like a swan, that's here and gone.
  C
A man gets tied up to the ground,
       G
He gives the world its saddest sound,
    Em
Its saddest sound.

Verse 2
    Em   **G**
I'd rather be a forest than a tree,
                    Em
Yes I would, if I could, I surely would.
                  G
I'd rather feel the earth beneath my feet,
                  Em
Yes I would, if I could, I surely would.

C	C	G	G	

Fade

C	C	G	G	Em	Em	

C'mon Everybody

Words & Music by Eddie Cochran & Jerry Capehart

```
  E          A          B7
```

Intro   ‖: E | A | B7 A | E :‖

                        E
Verse 1   Well come on everybody and let's get together tonight!

I got some money in my jeans and I'm really gonna spend it tonight!
               A   B7
Been a-doin' my homework all week long,
A   B7   E
Now the house is empty, the folks are gone.
N.C.
Ooo! Ooo! C'mon everybody!

Link   ‖: E | A | B7 A | E :‖

                        E
Verse 2   Well my baby's number one, but I'm gonna dance with three or four,

And the house'll be shakin' from the bare feet slappin' on the floor.
               A   B7
When you hear that music you just can't sit still,
               A   B7   E
If your brother won't rock then your sister will.
N.C.
Ooo! Ooo! C'mon everybody!

Link   ‖: E | A | B7 A | E :‖

Verse 3

                   E
Well we'll really have a party, but we gotta put a guard outside.

If the folks come home I'm afraid they're gonna have my hide.

        A   **B7**
There'll be no more movies for a week or two,

   A   **B7**   **E**
No more runnin' around with the usual crew.

N.C.
Ooo! Ooo! C'mon everybody!

Link   ‖: **E** | **A** | **B7** **A** | **E**   :‖ *Repeat to fade*

Eleanor Rigby

Words & Music by by John Lennon & Paul McCartney

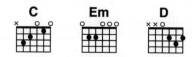

Chorus 1

C   Em
Ah, look at all the lonely people,
C   Em
Ah, look at all the lonely people.

Verse 1

Em
Eleanor Rigby

                    C
Picks up the rice in a church where a wedding has been,
     Em
Lives in a dream.

Waits at the window,

            D   C
Wearing a face that she keeps in a jar by the door,
    Em
Who is it for?

All the lonely people, where do they all come from?

All the lonely people, where do they all belong?

Verse 2

Em
Father McKenzie,

                   C
Writing the words of a sermon that no-one will hear,
    Em
No-one comes near.

Look at him working,

                      C
Darning his socks in the night when there's nobody there,
    Em
What does he care?

(cont.)

(Em)
All the lonely people, where do they all come from?

All the lonely people, where do they all belong?

Chorus 2

C   Em
Ah, look at all the lonely people,
C   Em
Ah, look at all the lonely people.

Verse 3

Em
Eleanor Rigby

                                       C
Died in the church and was buried along with her name,
      Em
Nobody came.

Father McKenzie,

                                             C
Wiping the dirt from his hands as he walks from the grave,
       Em
No-one was saved.

All the lonely people, where do they all come from?

All the lonely people, where do they all belong?

The First Cut Is The Deepest

Words & Music by Cat Stevens

Intro | G   D | C   D | G   D | C   D ||

Verse 1
              G   D   C   D
I would have given you all of my heart,
              G   D   C   D
But there's someone who's torn it apart,
              G   D   C
And she's taken almost all that I've got,
          D   G   D   C
But if you want I'll try to love again,
D   G   C   D
Baby I'll try to love again but I know

Chorus 1
G   D   C   D   G
The first cut is the deepest, baby I know,
           D   C   D
The first cut is the deepest.
             G   D   C   D
'Cos when it comes to being lucky she's cursed,
             G   C   D   C D
When it comes to loving me she's worst,
             G   D   C
But when it comes to being loved she's first,
          D
That's how I know
G   D   C   D   G
The first cut is the deepest, baby I know
           D   C   D
The first cut is the deepest.

Verse 2

       G   **D**   **C**   **D**
I still want you by my side,

       G   **D**   **D**   **C** **D**
Just to help me dry the tears that I've cried,

       G   **D**   **C**
'Cos I'm sure gonna give you a try,

     D   **G**   **D**   **C**
And if you want I'll try to love again,

    D **G**   **C**   **D**
But baby I'll try to love again but I know

Chorus 2

     G   **D**   **C**   **D**   **G**
‖: The first cut is the deepest, baby I know,

    D   **C**   **D**
The first cut is the deepest.

       G   **D**   **C**   **D**
'Cos when it comes to being lucky she's cursed,

     G   **C**   **D**   **C** **D**
When it comes to loving me she's worst,

     G   **D**   **C**
But when it comes to being loved she's first,

 D
That's how I know

G   **D**   **C**   **D**   **G**
The first cut is the deepest, baby I know

    D   **C**   **D**
The first cut is the deepest. :‖ *Repeat to fade*

Free To Decide

Words & Music by Dolores O'Riordan

G   C   Am

Intro   ‖: G | C | Am | Am   :‖

Verse 1

```
     G                    C
It's not worth anything more
            Am
Than this at all.
   G
I live as I choose
      C          Am
Or I will not live at all.
      G              C
So return to where you've come from,
     Am
Return to where you dwell,
                 G              C
Because her harassment's not my forté
          Am
But you do it very well.
```

Chorus 1

```
     G     C
I'm free to decide,
      Am
I'm free to decide,
         G
And I got so serious
C        Am
I had it all.
     G     C
I'm free to decide,
      Am
I'm free to decide,
         G
And I got so serious
C        Am            G
I died after all, it all, it all, it all.
```

Solo ‖: G | C | Am | Am :‖

Verse 2
      G   C
You must have nothing more

           Am
With your time to do.

         G
There's a war in Russia

     C   Am
And Sarajevo too.

     G   C
So to hell with what you're thinking,

        Am
And to hell with your narrow mind,

        G   C
You're so distracted from the real thing

        Am
You should leave your life behind, behind.

Chorus 2   As Chorus 1

    C Am   G   C   Am
Ee, ee, ah,— da,— da,— aa, da, da.

       G   C
Outro   I'm free to decide,

       Am
I'm free to decide,

       G
And I got so serious

  C   Am   G
I died after all, it all, it all, it all.

Solo ‖: G | C | Am | Am :‖ G ‖

Going Down

Words & Music by Ian Brown & John Squire

D   A   G

Intro
   | D | A | G | A ||

Verse 1

D   A
Dawn sings in the garden,

G   A
Phone sings in the hall,

D   A
This boy's dead from two days life

      G   A
Resurrected by the call.

Verse 2

D   A
Penny here, we've got to come,

     G   A
So come on round to me.

         D   A
There's so much, Penny, lying here

     G   A
To touch, taste and see.

Chorus 1

G   A
Ring a ding ding ding,

        D
I'm going down,

G   D | G ||
I'm coming round.

Verse 3

D   A
Penny's place, a crummy room,

     G   A
Her Dansette crackles to Jimi's tune.

D   A
I don't care, I taste Ambre Solaire,

     G   A
Her neck, her thighs, her lips, her hair.

Chorus 2   As Chorus 1

Bridge 1

A
All thoughts of sleep desert me,

D   G
There is no time,

A   G
Thirty minutes brings me round to

               A
Her number nine. ——

Solo | D | A | G | A   ‖

Verse 4

D   A
Yeah, she looks like a painting:

G   A
Jackson Pollock's number five.

     D   A
Come into the forest and taste the trees,

   G   A
The sun starts shining and I'm hard to please.

Chorus 3   As Chorus 1

Bridge 2   As Bridge 1

Verse 5

     G   D
So to look down on the clouds,

G   D
You don't need to fly.

G   A
I've never flown in a plane,

          D
I'll live until I die.

Johhny B. Goode

Words & Music by Chuck Berry

A   **D**   **E**

Intro | A | A | A | A |

| D | D | A | A |

| E | E | A | A   ‖

Verse 1
　　　　　　　　A
Deep down in Louisiana close to New Orleans,

Way back up in the woods among the evergreens,
　　　　　　　D
There stood a log cabin made of earth and wood
　　　　　　　A
Where lived a country boy named Johnny B. Goode
　　　　　　E
Who never ever learned to read or write so well
　　　　　　　A
But he could play a guitar just like a-ringing a bell.

Chorus 1
　　A
Go! Go! Go Johnny go,

Go, go Johnny go,
　D
Go, go Johnny go,
　A
Go, go Johnny go,
　E　　　　　　　A
Go! Johnny B. Goode.

Verse 2

          (A)
He used to carry his guitar in a gunny sack,

Go sit beneath the tree by the railroad track.

   D
Ol' engineer in the train sittin' in the shade

A
Strummin' with the rhythm that the drivers made.

    E
The people passin' by, they would stop and stay

       A
Oh my but that little country boy could play.

Chorus 2   As Chorus 1

Instrumental ‖: A | A | A | A |

              | D | D | A | A |

              | E | E | A | A :‖

Verse 3

          (A)
His mother told him "Someday you will be a man,

And you will be the leader of a big old band.

D
Many people coming from miles around

   A
To hear you play your music till the sun goes down,

E
Maybe someday your name'll be in lights

     A
A-saying JOHNNY B. GOODE TONIGHT."

Chorus 3   As Chorus 1

Long Tall Sally

Words & Music by Enotris Johnson, Richard Penniman & Robert Blackwell

G   C   D7

Verse 1

            G
I'm gonna tell Aunt Mary 'bout Uncle John,

He said he had the mis'ry but he got a lot of fun.
C   **G**   **D7**   **C**
Oh baby, yeah baby, wo-oo-oo baby,
        G
Some fun tonight.

Verse 2

      G
I saw Uncle John with Long Tall Sally,

He saw Aunt Mary coming and he jumped back in the alley.
C   **G**   **D7**   **C**
Oh baby, yeah baby, wo-oo-oo baby,
        G
Some fun tonight.

Instrumental

| G | G | G | G | |
| D7 | C | G | G D7 ‖ |

G	G	G	G	
C	C	G	G	
D7	C	G	G D7 ‖

Verse 3

      G
Well Long Tall Sally's built pretty sweet,

She got everything that Uncle John needs.
C   **G**   **D7**   **C**
Oh baby, yeah baby, wo-oo-oo baby,
        G
Some fun tonight.

Instrumental | G | G | G | G |
| C | C | G | G |
| D7 | C | G | G D7 ||

Coda

              G
We're gonna have some fun tonight,

Have some fun tonight,
C
Everything's alright,
G
Have some fun tonight,
D7   **C** **G**   **D7**
Have some fun, yeah, yeah, yeah.

              G
We're gonna have some fun tonight,

Have some fun tonight,
C
Everything's alright,
G
Have some fun tonight,
           D7   **C**   **G**
Yeah we'll have some fun,   some fun tonight.

Me And Julio
Down By The Schoolyard

Words & Music by Paul Simon

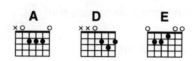

Intro　　𝄆 A　D ｜ A　E ｜ A　D ｜ A　E 𝄇　*Play 3 times*

Verse 1

      A
The mama pajama rolled out of bed
                  D
And she ran to the police station.
         E
When the papa found out, he began to shout
               A
And he started the investigation.
        E   A
It's against the law, it was against the law,
        E   A
What the mama saw, it was against the law.

Verse 2

      A
The mama looked down and spit on the ground
              D
Every time my name gets mentioned.
      E
The papa said "Oi, if I get that boy
                   A
I'm gonna stick him in the house of detention!"

Chorus 1

         D
Well I'm on my way,
      A
I don't know where I'm goin',
      D
I'm on my way,
      A   E
I'm taking my time but I don't know where.

        D   A
Goodbye Rosie, the Queen of Corona, see you

A   D   E   A   D A E
Me and Julio down by the schoolyard,

A   D   E   A   D A E
Me and Julio down by the schoolyard.

Instrumental
D	A	D	A E
D	A	A	D E	A D	A E
A	D E	A D	A E	E	

Verse 3
                A
Wo-oh! In a couple of days they come and take me away

                D
But the press let the story leak.

                E
And when the radical priest come to get me released

                A
We's all on the cover of Newsweek.

Chorus 2
                D
And I'm on my way,

                A
I don't know where I'm goin',

                D
I'm on my way,

                A   E
I'm taking my time but I don't know where.

                D   A   D A E
Goodbye Rosie, the Queen of Corona,   see you

A   D   E   A   D A E
Me and Julio down by the schoolyard,   see you

A   D   E   A   D A E
Me and Julio down by the schoolyard,   see you

A   D   E   A   D A E
Me and Julio down by the schoolyard.

Coda
‖: A D | A E | A D | A E :‖ *Repeat to fade*

Mr Tambourine Man

Words & Music by Bob Dylan

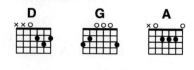

Intro | D | D ||

Chorus 1
    G   A   D   G
Hey Mister Tambourine Man play a song for me,
            D   G   A
I'm not sleepy and there is no place I'm going to.
    G   A   D   G
Hey Mister Tambourine Man play a song for me
            D   G   A   D
In the jingle-jangle morning I'll come following you.

Verse 1
            G   A   D   G
Though I know that evenin's empire has returned into sand,
    D   G
Vanished from my hand,
            D   G   A
Left me blindly here to stand but still not sleepin'.
    G   A   D   G
My weariness amazes me, I'm branded on my feet,
    D   G
I have no-one to meet
            D   G   A
And the ancient empty street's too dead for dreamin'.

Chorus 2   As Chorus 1

Verse 2

```
       G           A              D            G
Take me on a trip upon your magic swirlin' ship,
         D           G            D                G
My senses have been stripped, my hands can't feel to grip,
         D            G         D          G           A
My toes too numb to step, wait only for my boot heels to be wanderin'.
         G           A              D          G
I'm ready to go anywhere, I'm ready for to fade
      D          G              D            G
Into my own parade, cast your dancin' spell my way
                        A
I promise to go under it.
```

Chorus 3

```
    G           A            D             G
Hey Mister Tambourine Man play a song for me,
         D             G           A
I'm not sleepy and there is no place I'm going to.
G           A              D          G
Hey Mister Tambourine Man play a song for me
      D           G            A        D
In the jingle-jangle morning I'll come following you.
```

Verse 3

```
                    G               A            D            G
Though you might hear laughin' spinnin' swingin' madly across the sun,
         D          G          D          G
It's not aimed at anyone, it's just escapin' on the run
         D           G          A
And but for the sky there are no fences facin'.
      G              A        D            G
And if you hear vague traces of skippin' reels of rhyme
       D          G            D           G
To your tambourine in time, it's just a ragged clown behind,
            D         G          D
I wouldn't pay it any mind, it's just a shadow you're
G            A
Seein' that he's chasin'.
```

Chorus 4   As Chorus 3

Instrumental | G A | D G | D G | D G |
Verse 3

| D G | D G | D G | A |

| G A | D G | D G | D G |

| D G | A D | D   ‖

Verse 4

      G   A   D   G
Then take me disappearin' through the smoke rings of my mind

          D   G   D   G
Down the foggy ruins of time, far past the frozen leaves,

       D   G   D   G
The haunted, frightened trees out to the windy beach

       D   G   A
Far from the twisted reach of crazy sorrow.

        G   A   D   G
Yes, to dance beneath the diamond sky with one hand wavin' free

         D   G   D   G
Silhouetted by the sea, circled by the circus sands

         D   G   D   G
With all memory and fate driven deep beneath the waves

         D   G   A
Let me forget about today until tomorrow.

Chorus 5

G   A   D   G
Hey Mister Tambourine Man play a song for me,

       D   G   A
I'm not sleepy and there is no place I'm going to.

G   A   D   G
Hey Mister Tambourine Man play a song for me

       D   G   A   D
In the jingle-jangle morning I'll come following you.

Mull Of Kintyre

Words & Music by McCartney & Laine

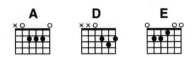

Chorus 1

A
Mull of Kintyre,

  D   **A**
Oh mist rolling in from the sea,

    D
My desire is always to be here,

  A
Oh Mull of Kintyre.

Verse 1

(A)
Far have I travelled and much have I seen,

D   **A**
Dark distant mountains and valleys of green,

A
Past painted deserts, the sunset's on fire

    D   **E**   **A**
As he carries me home to the Mull of Kintyre.

Chorus 2 As Chorus 1

Verse 2

(A)
Sweep through the heather like deer in the glen,

D   **A**
Carry me back to the days I knew then.

A
Nights when we sang like a heavenly choir

    D   **E**   **A**
Of the life and the times of the Mull of Kintyre.

Chorus 3 As Chorus 1

Oh Boy

Words & Music by Sunny West, Bill Tilghman & Norman Petty

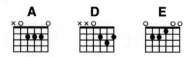

Verse 1

    A
All of my love, all of my kissing,

You don't know what you've been a-missing.

Chorus 1

    D
Oh boy (oh boy,) when you're with me,
   A
Oh boy (oh boy,) the world can see
   E   D   A D A E
That you were meant for me.

Verse 2

    A
All of my life I've been waiting,

Tonight there'll be no hesitating.

Chorus 2

    D
Oh boy (oh boy,) when you're with me,
   A
Oh boy (oh boy,) the world can see
   E   D   A D A
That you were meant for me.

Bridge 1

E
Stars appear and shadows are falling,
A
You can hear my heart a-calling,
   D
A little bit of loving makes everything right,
E
I'm gonna see my baby toight.

Verse 3

As Verse 1

Chorus 3	As Chorus 1					
Instrumental	| A	| A	| A	| A	| D	| D	|
	| A	| A	| E	| D	| A	| E	||

Verse 4   As Verse 1

Chorus 4   As Chorus 1

Verse 5   As Verse 2

Chorus 5   As Chorus 2

Bridge 2   As Bridge 1

Verse 6   As Verse 1

Chorus 6   As Chorus 1

Paperback Writer

Words & Music by John Lennon & Paul McCartney

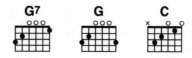

Intro

N.C.
Paperback writer, paperback writer.

| G7 | G7 | G7 | G7 ‖

Verse 1

          G
Dear Sir or Madam, could you read my book,
            G7   G
It took me years to write, could you take a look?

It's based on a novel by a man named Lear
          G7   G   C
And I need a job, so I want to be a paperback writer,
          G
Paperback writer.

Verse 2

          (G)
It's a dirty story of a dirty man
          G7   G
And his clinging wife doesn't understand.

His son is working for the Daily Mail,
          G7   G   C
It's a steady job but he wants to be a paperback writer,
          G
Paperback writer.

Chorus 1

N.C.
Paperback writer, paperback writer.

| G7 | G7 | G7 | G7 ‖

Verse 3

 G
It's a thousand pages give or take a few,
 G7   **G**
I'll be writing more in a week or two,

I can make it longer if you like the style,
 G7   **G**   **C**
I can change it round and I want to be a paperback writer,
    G
Paperback writer.

Verse 4

 (G)
If you really like it you can have the rights,
 G7   **G**
It could make a million for you overnight.

If you must return it you can send it here
 G7   **G**   **C**
But I need a break and I want to be a paperback writer,
    G
Paperback writer.

Chorus 2

 N.C.
Paperback writer, paperback writer

| **G7** | **G7** | **G7** | **G7** ‖

Coda

‖: **G**
Paperback writer, (paperback writer,) :‖ *Repeat to fade*

The Mighty Quinn

Words & Music by Bob Dylan

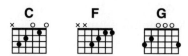

    C   F   G

Verse 1

    C   F   C   F
Ev'rybody's building the big ships and the boats,

    C   F
Some are building monuments,

    C   F
Others jotting down notes.

    C   F
Ev'rybody's in despair,

    C   F
Ev'ry girl and boy but when

  C   G
Quinn The Eskimo gets here,

       F   C
Ev'rybody's gonna jump for joy.

Chorus 1

  (C)   G   C
Come all without, come all within,

            G   F   C
You'll not see nothing like the mighty Quinn.

  E   G   C
Come all without, come all within,

            G   F   C
You'll not see nothing like the mighty Quinn.

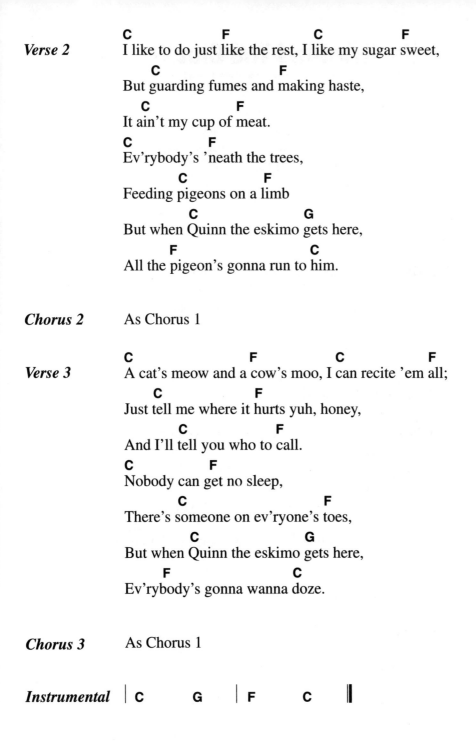

Verse 2

    C   F   C   F
I like to do just like the rest, I like my sugar sweet,

      C   F
But guarding fumes and making haste,

      C   F
It ain't my cup of meat.

    C   F
Ev'rybody's 'neath the trees,

        C   F
Feeding pigeons on a limb

          C   G
But when Quinn the eskimo gets here,

      F   C
All the pigeon's gonna run to him.

Chorus 2   As Chorus 1

Verse 3

    C   F   C   F
A cat's meow and a cow's moo, I can recite 'em all;

      C   F
Just tell me where it hurts yuh, honey,

        C   F
And I'll tell you who to call.

    C   F
Nobody can get no sleep,

        C   F
There's someone on ev'ryone's toes,

          C   G
But when Quinn the eskimo gets here,

      F   C
Ev'rybody's gonna wanna doze.

Chorus 3   As Chorus 1

Instrumental | C   G | F   C   ‖

Rock Around The Clock

Words & Music by Max C. Freedman & Jimmy de Knight

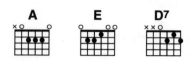

Intro

A
One, two, three o'clock, four o'clock rock,

Five, six, seven o'clock, eight o'clock rock,

Nine, ten, eleven o'clock, twelve o'clock rock,
E
We're gonna rock around the clock tonight!

Verse 1

A
Put your glad rags on and join me, Hon,

We'll have some fun when the clock strikes one,
D7
We're gonna rock around the clock tonight,
A
We're gonna rock, rock, rock 'til broad daylight,
E   **A**
We're gonna rock, gonna rock, around the clock tonight.

Verse 2

(A)
When the clock strikes two, and three and four,

If the band slows down we'll ask for more,
D7
We're gonna rock around the clock tonight,
A
We're gonna rock, rock, rock 'til broad daylight,
E   **A**
We're gonna rock, gonna rock, around the clock tonight.

Instrumental | A | A | A | A | D7 | D7 |

| A | A | E | E | A | A ‖

Verse 3

(A)
When the chimes ring five, six and seven,

We'll be ridin' seventh heaven,

D7
We're gonna rock around the clock tonight,

A
We're gonna rock, rock, rock 'til broad daylight,

E   A
We're gonna rock, gonna rock, around the clock tonight.

Verse 4

(A)
When it's eight, nine, ten, eleven too,

I'll be goin' strong and so will you,

D7
We're gonna rock around the clock tonight,

A
We're gonna rock, rock, rock 'til broad daylight,

E   A
We're gonna rock, gonna rock, around the clock tonight.

Instrumental | A | A | A | A | D7 | D7 |

| A | A | E | E | A | A ||

Verse 5

(A)
When the clock strikes twelve, we'll cool off, then

Start a-rockin' round the clock again,

D7
We're gonna rock around the clock tonight,

A
We're gonna rock, rock, rock 'til broad daylight,

E   A
We're gonna rock, gonna rock, around the clock tonight.

Spice Up Your Life

Words & Music by Geri Halliwell, Emma Bunton, Melanie Brown,
Melanie Chisholm, Victoria Aadams, Richard Stannard & Matt Rowe

Em   B7   B

Intro

‖: Em   B7
La la la la la la, la la la,

Em   B7
La la la la la la, la la la. :‖

Verse 1

Em   B7
When you're feeling sad and low

Em   B7
We will take you where you gotta go.

Em   B7
Smiling, dancing, everything is free,

Em   B7
All you need is positivity.

Pre-chorus 1

Em
Colours of the world (spice up your life)

      B
Every boy and every girl (spice up your life)

Em
People of the world (spice up your life)

B
Ah!

Chorus 1

Em
Slam it to the left (if you're having a good time)

B7
Shake it to the right (if you know that you feel fine)

Em
Chicas to the front, uh, uh,

   B7
Go round.

Em
Slam it to the left (if you're having a good time)

B7
Shake it to the right (if you know that you feel fine)

(contd)
Em
Chicas to the front, uh, uh,

B7
Hi-ci-ya hold tight!

‖: Em   B7
La la la la la la, la la la,
Em   B7
La la la la la la, la la la.   :‖

Verse 2
Em   B7
Yellow man in Timbuktu,
Em   B7
Colour for both me and you.
Em   B7
Kung-Fu fighting, dancing queen,
Em   B7
Tribal spaceman and all that's in between.

Pre-chorus 2   As Pre-chorus 1

Chorus 2   As Chorus 1

Bridge
(spoken)
Em   B7
Flamenco lambada but hip hop is harder,
Em   B7
We moonwalk the foxtrot, then polka the salsa.
Em
Shake it, shake it, shake it haka!
B7
Shake it, shake it, shake it haka!
Em   B7
Ariba!

Pre-chorus 3   As Pre-chorus 1

Outro   ‖: As Chorus 1 :‖

Still Water

Words & Music by Frank Wilson & William 'Smokey' Robinson

D   **Bm**   **A**

| D | Bm | A | A ‖

Intro   *Spoken:* Walk with me,   take my hand.

‖: D | Bm | A | A :‖   *Play 3 times*

       D   **Bm** | A | A |

Sung: Still water! Still water!

D   **Bm**   **A**
Ah, __ ah, __ ah. __

               D   **Bm**

Verse 1   Never you mind if I

          A
Don't tell strangers passing by,

         D
If I don't brag,

           Bm
If I don't brag or boast,

         A
Click my glass and say a toast

     D   **Bm**
About my love for you,

       A
How it'll run so deep and true,

D   **Bm**
And that is so,

A
 'Cos you don't know

D   **Bm**
Still waters run deep,

A
Still waters run deep,

D   **Bm**
Still waters run deep,

A
Still waters run deep.

Verse 2 ‖: D | Bm | A | A   :‖

| D | Bm | A | A   ‖

Take my hand.

Outro

‖: **D**
Still water!

Bm   **A**
Running deep take my hand,

Woh-oh-oh now,

D   **Bm**
Still waters run deep,

A
Hey, hey, hey!   :‖   *Repeat to fade*

Walk Of Life

Words & Music by Mark Knopfler

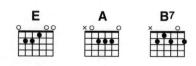

Intro ‖: E | A | B7 | A B7 :‖ *Pay 4 times*

Verse 1
E
Here comes Johnny singing oldies, goldies,

Be bop a lula, baby what I say.

Here comes Johnny singing 'I got a woman'

Down in the tunnels trying to make it pay.

Pre-chorus 1
A
He got the action, he got the motion,
E
Oh yeah, the boy can play.
A
Dedication, devotion,
E
Turning all the night-time into the day.

Chorus 1
E   B7
He do the song about the sweet-loving woman,
        E   A
He do the song about the knife,
            E   B7   A
Then he do the walk, he do the walk of life,
B7   E
Yeah he do the walk of life.

Link 1 | E | A | B7 | A B7 ‖

Verse 2

E
Here comes Johnny, gonna tell you a story,

Hand me down my walking shoes.

Here comes Johnny with the power and the glory,

Backbeat, the talking blues.

Pre-chorus 2   As Pre-chorus 1

Chorus 2   As Chorus 1

Link 2   ‖: E | A | B7 | A   B7 :‖

Verse 3

E
Here comes Johnny singing oldies, goldies,

Be bop a lula, baby what I say.

Here comes Johnny singing 'I got a woman'

Down in the tunnels trying to make it pay.

Pre-chorus 3
     (E)   B7
And after all the violence and doubletalk,
         E   A
There's just a song in all the trouble and the strife.

Chorus 3   As Chorus 1

Link 3   ‖: E | A | B7 | A   B7 :‖   *Repeat to fade*

Ride A White Swan

Words & Music by Marc Bolan

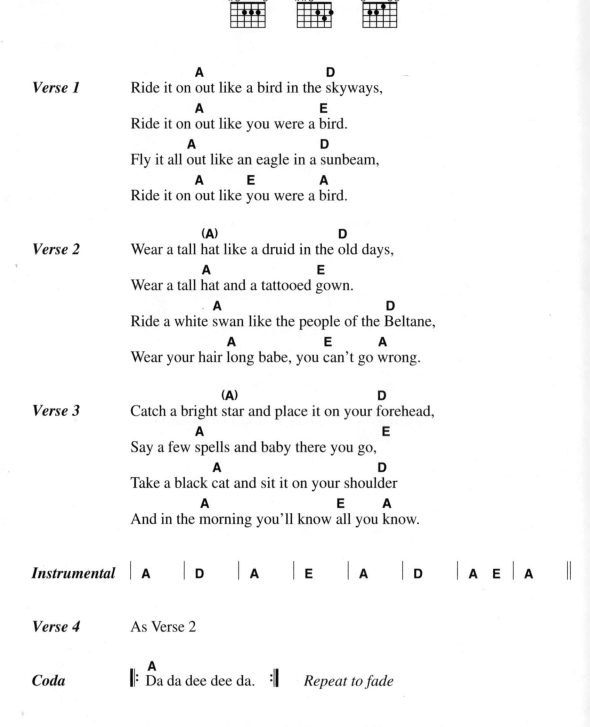

Verse 1

      A   D
Ride it on out like a bird in the skyways,
      A   E
Ride it on out like you were a bird.
      A   D
Fly it all out like an eagle in a sunbeam,
      A   E   A
Ride it on out like you were a bird.

Verse 2

          (A)   D
Wear a tall hat like a druid in the old days,
          A   E
Wear a tall hat and a tattooed gown.
          A   D
Ride a white swan like the people of the Beltane,
          A   E   A
Wear your hair long babe, you can't go wrong.

Verse 3

          (A)   D
Catch a bright star and place it on your forehead,
          A   E
Say a few spells and baby there you go,
          A   D
Take a black cat and sit it on your shoulder
          A   E   A
And in the morning you'll know all you know.

Instrumental | A | D | A | E | A | D | A E | A ||

Verse 4   As Verse 2

Coda ||: Da da dee dee da. :|| *Repeat to fade*

2/01 (39584)